CONTENTS

Recorded by JIM CROCE

TIME IN A BOTTLE

Words and Music by
JIM CROCE

Recorded by JIM CROCE

BAD, BAD LEROY BROWN

Words and Music by
JIM CROCE

6

7

Recorded by JIM CROCE

I GOT A NAME

Words by
NORMAN GIMBEL

Music by
CHARLES FOX

1. Like the pine trees lin - ing the wind - ing road,
2. Like the north wind whis - tl - in' down the sky,
3. (Instrumental)
4. Like the fool I am and I'll al - ways be,

I've got a name; I've got a name.
I've got a song; I've got a song.
(Instrumental)
I've got a dream; I've got a dream.

Like the sing - ing bird and the croak - ing
Like the whip - poor - will and the ba - by's
(Instrumental
They can change their minds but they can't change

Recorded by JIM CROCE

I'LL HAVE TO SAY I LOVE YOU IN A SONG

Words and Music by
JIM CROCE

1. Well, I know it's kind of late — I hope I did-n't wake you,
2. (Yeah, I) know it's kind of strange — but ev-'ry time I'm near you,
3. (Instrumental)

But what I got to say can't wait — I know you'd un-der-stand.
I just run out of things to say — I know you'd un-der-stand.

Chorus:

1.2.4. Ev-'ry time I tried to tell ___ you the words just came out wrong. So I'll
3. Ev-'ry time the time was right ___ all the words just came out wrong. So I'll

Recorded by JIM CROCE

WORKIN' AT THE CAR WASH BLUES

Words and Music by
JIM CROCE

Moderately, with a funky beat

15

16

Recorded by JIM CROCE

YOU DON'T MESS AROUND WITH JIM

Words and Music by
JIM CROCE

Recorded by JIM CROCE

ONE LESS SET OF FOOTSTEPS

Words and Music by
JIM CROCE

Lyrics under the staff:

We been run-nin' a-way__ from some-thin' we both know, We've

long run out of things to say__ and I think I bet-ter go.__

Recorded by JIM CROCE

IT DOESN'T HAVE TO BE THAT WAY

Words and Music by
JIM CROCE

'Cause we could eas-i-ly get it to-geth-er to-night,_____

It's on-ly right._____

Verse Crowd-ed stores,__ the cor-ner San-ta Claus, Tin-sled af-ter-noons;__

_____ And the side-walk bands__ that play their songs__

D7 G7 C Cmaj7
Slight-ly out of tune. On the wind - y win - ter
C6 C F Em Dm7 G7
av - e - nues, There walks a lone - ly man; And
C Cmaj7 C6 C F G7 C G7
if I told you who he is, Well, I think you'd un - der - stand. But it
mf
D. S. al Coda
Coda
C Dm7 Em F G7 C
rall.

Recorded by JIM CROCE

FIVE SHORT MINUTES

Words and Music by
JIM CROCE

Be - cause five short min - utes of love _____ will cost me

twen - ty long years ___ in jail. _____ 2. Well, like a

fool in a hur - ry I took her to my room, She cast - ed me in plas - ter while I

sang her a tune, ___ Then I said, ooh, _____ oo - ee, _____ sure was a trag - ic tale, ___

Recorded by JIM CROCE

ROLLER DERBY QUEEN

Moderate beat

Words and Music by
JIM CROCE

1. Gon-na tell you a sto-ry that you won't be-lieve,___ But I fell in love___ last Fri-day eve-nin' With a girl I saw___ on a bar-room T. V. screen.___ Well, I was just get-tin' read-y to get___

* Play all ♩♪ as ♩.♪

Additional Verses

2. She's a five—foot—six and two-fifteen,
   A bleached blonde mama with a streak of mean;
   She knew how to knuckle
   And she knew how to scuffle and fight.
   And the Roller Derby program said
   That she were built like a 'frigerator with a head,
   The fans called her "Tuffy,"
   But all her buddies called her "Spike." *(Chorus)*

3. Well, I could not help but fall in love
   With this heavy duty woman I been speakin' of;
   Things looked kind of bad
   Until the day she skated into my life.
   Well, she might be nasty, she might be fat,
   But I never met a person who would tell her that;
   She's my big blonde bomber,
   My heavy-handed Hackensack Mama. *(Chorus)*

Recorded by JIM CROCE

THE MAN THAT IS ME

Words and Music by
JIM and INGRID CROCE

Words and Music by
JIM CROCE and INGRID CROCE

42

Recorded by JIM CROCE

ALABAMA RAIN

Words and Music by
JIM CROCE

On a dust-y mid-Ju-ly,___ Coun-try sum-mer's eve - nin';___

A weep-in' wil - low sang its lul - la - by___ and shared our se - cret.___

D. S. al Coda

Coda

rain.___ Walk-in' in the

Al - a - bam - a rain._____

rall.

Recorded by JIM CROCE

SPEEDBALL TUCKER

Words and Music by
JIM CROCE

Moderately bright beat

I drive a

broke-down rig___ on "may-pop" tires,___ For - ty foot of o - ver - load;___
rain may blow,___ the snow may snow,___ And the turn - pikes___ they may freeze;___

___ A lot of peo - ple say that I'm cra - zy, Be - cause I
___ But that don't both - er ol' Speed - ball, He go - in'

3. One day I looked into my rear view mirror
   And a-comin' up from behind
   There was a Georgia State policeman
   And a hundred dollar fine.
   Well, he looked me in the eye as he was writin' me up
   And said, "Driver, you been flyin'
   And ninety-five was the route you were on
   It was not the speed limit sign."

Recorded by JIM CROCE

PHOTOGRAPHS AND MEMORIES

Words and Music by
JIM CROCE

51

Recorded by JIM CROCE

RAPID ROY
(The Stock Car Boy)

Words and Music by
JIM CROCE

Rap-id Roy __ that stock __ car boy, __ He too much to __ be-lieve; __ You know he al-ways got an ex-tra pack of cig-a-rettes, Rolled up __ in his T - shirt sleeve. __ He got a tat-too on his arms that say "Ba - by." He got an-

Recorded by JIM CROCE

BIG WHEEL

Words and Music by
JIM CROCE

Recorded by JIM CROCE

ANOTHER DAY, ANOTHER TOWN

Words and Music by
JIM CROCE

Recorded by JIM CROCE

OPERATOR
(That's Not The Way It Feels)

Words and Music by
JIM CROCE

tell them I'm fine and to show_____ I've o-ver-come the blow, I've learned to take it well,___

_____ I on-ly wish my words___ could just con-vince my-self_____ That it just was-n't real,___

But that's not the way it feels.

2. Operator, could you help me place this call?
   'Cause I can't read the number that you just gave me
   There's something in my eyes,
   You know it happens every time;
   I think about the love that I thought would save me.

   (Chorus)

3. Operator, let's forget about this call,
   There's no one there I really wanted to talk to.
   Thank you for your time,
   'Cause you've been so much more than kind
   And you can keep the dime.

   (Chorus)